FROM TRASH TO TREASURE

NATURE CRAFTS

by Ruth Owen

PowerKiDS press

New York

Published in 2014 by The Rosen Publishing Group, Inc.
29 East 21st Street, New York, NY 10010

First Edition

Produced for Rosen by Ruby Tuesday Books Ltd
Editor for Ruby Tuesday Books Ltd: Mark J. Sachner
US Editor: Joshua Shadowens
Designer: Emma Randall

Photo Credits:
Cover, 1, 3, 4–5, 6–7, 8–9, 10, 13 (top), 14, 18, 26, 30–31 © Shutterstock; cover, 1, 10–11, 12, 13 (bottom), 15, 16–17, 19, 20–21, 22–23, 24–25, 27, 28–29, 30–31 © Ruth Owen and John Such.

Publisher Cataloging Data

Owen, Ruth.
Nature crafts / by Ruth Owen.
  p. cm. — (From trash to treasure)
Includes index.
ISBN 978-1-4777-1285-6 (library binding) — ISBN 978-1-4777-1364-8 (pbk.) — ISBN 978-1-4777-1365-5 (6-pack)
1. Nature craft—Juvenile literature. 2. Handicraft—Juvenile literature. I. Owen, Ruth, 1967– II. Title.
TT157.O94 2014
745.58—dc23

Manufactured in the United States of America

CPSIA Compliance Information: Batch #S13PK8: For Further Information contact Rosen Publishing, New York, New York at 1-800-237-9932

CONTENTS

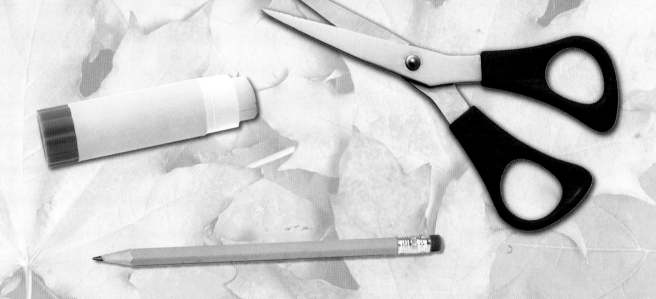

REDUCE, REUSE, RECYCLE

Every year in the United States, so much trash is produced that it amounts to over 1,600 pounds (725 kg) of garbage for every person in the country.

In fact, while the United States is home to only 5 percent of the world's people, it produces around 40 percent of the world's trash! With much of that trash simply being dumped into **landfills**, it's more important than ever to find ways to live by the three Rs—reduce, reuse, and **recycle**.

If you're reading this book, you probably already recycle materials such as paper, plastic, and glass. You can also reuse many things, however. From bottle tops to old spoons and forks, to DVDs and rubber boots, it's possible to turn trash into **environmentally friendly** new things that will help nature and look great in your backyard or garden.

The three Rs stand for reducing the amount of trash you make, reusing items instead of throwing them away, and recycling whenever you can.

4

You may not have space to create a life-size plastic bottle elephant sculpture in your backyard, but you can turn one of your family's recycled bottles into a bird feeder.

During an average American's lifetime, that person will create 600 times his or her adult weight in trash. Much of this trash will end up in a landfill site like the one in this photograph.

OLD BOOT PLANT POTS

You won't have a box or special recycling container in your house for old or unwanted boots. This doesn't mean, however, that you can't give your family's old boots a second life.

If boots or shoes are still in good condition, but are just too small or no longer wanted, you can give them to a thrift shop. These shops are usually run by **charities** that raise funds for their work by selling secondhand goods.

Another great way to reuse old rubber boots or hiking boots, however, is to turn them into funky plant pots for your garden. Colorful rubber boots make a great container for spring bulbs such as daffodils!

You will need:

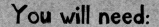

- A pair of old boots
- An ice pick
- A small spade
- Gravel
- Potting soil
- Small plants or bulbs
- A craft knife

STEP 1:

To plant spring bulbs in old rubber boots, begin by making six holes in the bottom of each boot with the ice pick. To stay safe, ask an adult to help you do this. The holes will allow rainwater to escape from the boots so the soil and bulbs don't get too wet.

STEP 2:

Completely fill the toes of the boots with gravel.

Holes to let water escape

STEP 3:

Fill the bottom of the boot with a layer of gravel about 1 inch (2.5 cm) deep.

STEP 4:
Add about 2 inches (5 cm) of potting soil on top of the gravel. The soil should reach ankle level inside the boots.

Fill with soil to here

STEP 5:
Place three daffodil bulbs on top of the soil in each boot. Cover the bulbs with soil up to about 1 inch (2.5 cm) from the top of the boot.

STEP 6:
Sprinkle a thin layer of gravel on top of the soil. Place the boots outside away from direct sunlight and wait for spring!

STEP 7:

You can also plant small plants in a pair of hiking boots by repeating steps 1 to 4. The soil will reach nearly to the top of the boots' ankles, and you can plant small plants in the soil.

STEP 8:

Ask an adult to help you cut a hole in the top of the toe of each boot, using a craft knife, and you can replace some of the gravel in the toe with soil and add some small plants here, too.

If made from leather or rubber, your **unique** boot plant containers will last for several years outside.

LADYBUG HERB POTS

Every year, about 25 billion plastic bottles are thrown away in the United States. That means 25 billion plastic bottle tops become trash, too.

Add to this waste plastic yogurt or soup containers, cardboard or plastic soda cups, and other food containers, and you have a mountain of trash. All of these items can be used, however, to make plant pots for growing **herbs**, seeds, and other small plants.

Just take a yogurt carton and some red bottle tops, and you can make an eye-catching ladybug plant pot. Add a **fragrant** herb plant to your pot, and you have a cute, cheap-to-make, and very green gift to give to a cook or gardener.

You will need:

- Empty plastic food and drink containers
- Scissors or an ice pick
- Waterproof paint
- A paintbrush
- Red plastic bottle tops
- Black paint or a black marker
- Googly eyes
- A glue gun
- Potting soil
- A small spade
- Small potted herbs from a garden center or supermarket

STEP 1:

Take a plastic container, a soda cup, or the bottom from a plastic bottle, and make five pea-sized holes in the bottom of the container using an ice pick or scissors. For safety, ask an adult to help you do this.

The holes will allow water to escape from the pot so the soil doesn't become waterlogged.

STEP 2:

Paint the container in the color of your choice. To add texture to your pot, mix a little sand into the paint.

This white paint has sand added for texture.

STEP 3:
Take a red plastic bottle top, and draw or paint on the ladybug's black head.

STEP 4:
Add a thick black line from the ladybug's head to create the wings. Then add black spots. Finally, glue on googly eyes.

STEP 5:
Make as many ladybugs as you wish to cover your pot. To stick the ladybugs to the pot, squeeze a circle of glue the size of a ladybug onto the pot and press the ladybug into the glue. Be careful not to get the hot glue on your fingers.

STEP 6:

Half fill the ladybug pot with potting soil. Place your herb plant into the pot and fill the pot with soil. Your recycled ladybug herb pot is complete!

THYME

ROSEMARY

BASIL

BOTTLE BIRD FEEDER

An average US family drinks 182 gallons (689 l) of soda, 104 gallons (394 l) of milk, 29 gallons (110 l) of juice, and 26 gallons (98 l) of bottled water each year. That adds up to a huge number of plastic bottles!

Thankfully, all of these bottles can be recycled. They can even be given a second life in a craft project before they are tossed into the recycling bin.

So, pull a plastic bottle from your family's recyclables, and use it to make a bird feeder. Birds will visit outdoor feeders all year long, but during winter, when there are no seeds or insects around to eat, your homemade bird feeder will become an important source of food to these wild creatures.

You will need:

- An empty plastic bottle with a cap
- Scissors or a craft knife
- 2 wooden spoons (you can recycle old spoons or buy them from a craft store)
- Wild bird seed
- String
- Twigs, bark, and moss for decoration

STEP 1:

About 2 inches (5 cm) up from the bottom of the bottle, cut an arch-shaped hole. The bottom of the arch shape should be just smaller than the width of the wooden spoon's bowl.

Approximate shape and size of hole to be cut in bottle

STEP 2:

Make a second, pea-sized hole in the bottle, directly opposite the arch-shaped hole.

Cut arch-shaped hole here

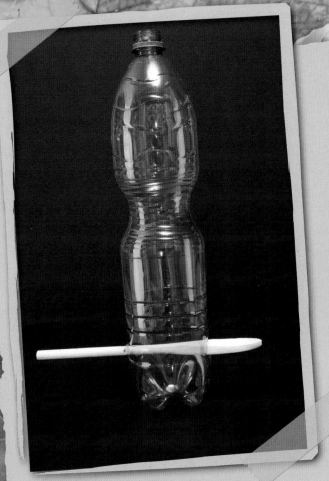

STEP 3:
Then, push the wooden spoon into the bottle through the arch-shaped hole. Thread the spoon's handle out again through the smaller hole.

STEP 4:
Repeat steps 1 to 3 about 5 inches (12.5 cm) from the top of the bottle.

Birds can stand here to feed.

Birds can perch here as they wait their turn!

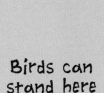

STEP 5:
Fill the bottle with wild bird seed and screw on the cap to stop rainwater from getting into the bottle. The seeds will spill out onto the wooden spoons, allowing small birds to feed on them.

STEP 6:

Tie a piece of string tightly around the neck of the bottle and hang your feeder outside. Choose a place that cats can't reach so the birds won't be attacked as they feed.

STEP 7:

If you wish, you can collect twigs, bark, and moss and glue these to the bottle to add decoration and help the feeder blend into the natural environment.

DVD PLANT LABELS

About four million CDs used in computers are thrown away every day in the United States. Add to that number unwanted or damaged DVDs and music CDs, and you have a massive quantity of unwanted plastic.

Unfortunately the type of plastic used to **manufacture** these discs can't be recycled along with your family's plastic bottles and other food packaging. So, most of these discs are thrown into the garbage and end up in landfills where they will take about 500 years to **degrade**!

These tough discs can be put to good use, however, in craft projects. For example, they can be reused and turned into funky plant labels to use in the garden.

You will need:

- Unwanted CDs or DVDs
- Chalkboard paint
- A paintbrush
- Beads or pebbles for decoration
- A glue gun
- Chalk or a waterproof chalkboard marker

STEP 1:

Paint the disc with chalkboard paint.

You will then be able to write the names of plants onto the disc using chalk or a waterproof chalkboard marker if the plant label needs to be more weatherproof.

STEP 2:
Allow the paint to dry.

STEP 3:

You can now decorate the edge of the disc. Squeeze a small blob of glue onto the disc and gently press on a pebble or bead. Be careful not to touch the hot glue with your fingers.

WARNING
Only use a glue gun if an adult is there to help you.

STEP 4:

Only stick decorations to one half of the disc, as the other half will be in the soil. You can use small pebbles from the garden for a natural look, or use buttons and beads from old clothes or jewelry for a more colorful design.

STEP 5:

When the glue has dried, your plant label is ready to use. Write the name of the plant you want to label.

STEP 6:

Press the lower half of the disc into the soil in a plant container or directly into a flowerbed, and your plants are labeled!

You can reuse your plant label again and again by wiping off the chalk, or by removing the words written in chalkboard marker using a cleaning product.

FORK AND SPOON WIND CHIMES

If you're passionate about recycling, it can be frustrating when something old is due to be thrown away and there is nowhere to send it.

Of course, there's always the option of sending items to a thrift shop so that a charity can make some money, and someone else who cares about reusing can buy something they need for just a few dollars. The other option is to take a look at the item and think how it could be **upcycled**. Just because those old forks and spoons used to live in the silverware drawer, it doesn't mean they can't now have a new life as a funky garden wind chime!

You will need:

- 10 to 12 old forks and spoons
- A wire coat hanger
- A set of wire cutters or pliers
- String
- Beads for decoration

STEP 1:

Unbend the coat hanger from its original shape. Cut off a piece of wire about 24 inches (60 cm) long.

STEP 2:

Bend the wire into a circle that's about 7 inches (18 cm) in diameter. Twist the two ends of the wire around each other to close the circle. You might need an adult's help to cut, bend, and twist the wire.

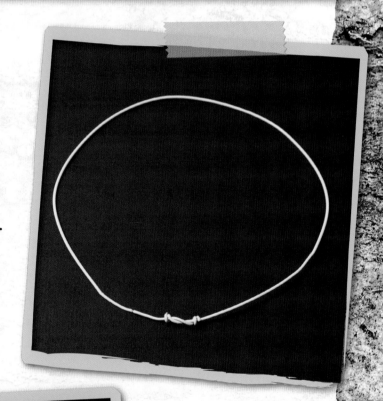

STEP 3:

Choose 10 to 12 forks and spoons to use. For each item, cut a length of string that's about 12 to 15 inches (30–38 cm) long.

STEP 4:
Tie a piece of string onto each fork or spoon by wrapping the string twice around the item's handle and tying it in a double knot.

STEP 5:
Now tie the individual forks and spoons onto the wire ring. Space the items evenly around the ring. Make some items hang lower or higher than others, but make sure that when pushed, each item will swing and touch the item next to it.

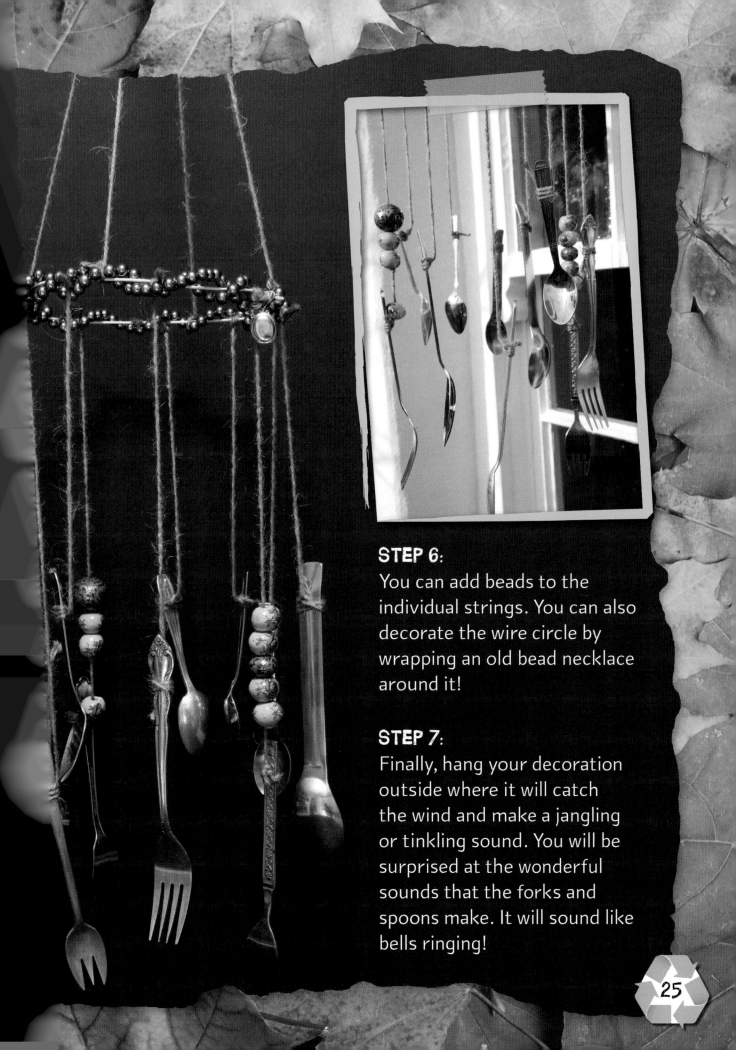

STEP 6:
You can add beads to the individual strings. You can also decorate the wire circle by wrapping an old bead necklace around it!

STEP 7:
Finally, hang your decoration outside where it will catch the wind and make a jangling or tinkling sound. You will be surprised at the wonderful sounds that the forks and spoons make. It will sound like bells ringing!

RECYCLED OUTDOOR LIGHT

Next time you're having a late barbecue or eating dinner outside, light up your night by making these pretty outdoor lights with recycled glass jars.

Glass can be a very green material because it can be recycled again and again into new glass items. If a glass jar ends up in a landfill, however, it could be in the ground for thousands of years before it breaks down. So recycle some small glass jam or pickle jars, used tissue paper and silver foil, and make these pretty candleholders.

You will need:

- Small, clean recycled glass jars
- Gently used tissue paper
- Scissors
- White glue
- A paintbrush
- Candle stubs or tea lights
- Garden wire
- A pencil
- A set of wire cutters or pliers
- Clean, recycled aluminum foil
- A skewer or knitting needle

STEP 1:
Cut out shapes, such as squares, from tissue paper.

STEP 2:
Using the paintbrush, brush some glue onto the outside of the jar. Stick the pieces of tissue paper to the jar. Overlap differently colored pieces of tissue paper for a layered effect.

STEP 3:
When the jar is covered with tissue paper, gently brush more glue over the top of the paper. When the glue has dried, your candleholder is ready to use.

STEP 4:

If you want to hang your candleholders from a tree branch or porch, take a piece of garden wire about 48 inches (122 cm) long. Bend the wire in half to create a loop. Place a pencil into the loop and twist five times. You will have made a small hoop.

STEP 5:

Holding the two ends of the wire, pull the hoop tight against the rim of the jar and then wrap the two ends of the wire around the rim twice—as if you were wrapping a scarf around a person's neck.

STEP 6:

Twist the two ends of wire together, put a pencil against the twist, and once again twist five times. Trim off the long ends of wire, and you now have a small hoop on the other side of the jar.

STEP 7:

You can now thread another piece of wire (or string) through the two hoops to make a handle so the candleholder can be hung up. First thread one end of the wire through one hoop.

STEP 8:

To decorate the handle, make beads by rolling up used, but clean, foil into small balls. Use a skewer or knitting needle to make a hole in the foil beads, and thread the hanging wire through the beads.

STEP 9:

Finally, thread the loose end of the hanging wire through the other loop on the jar, and the candleholder is ready to hang.

GLOSSARY

charities (CHER-uh-teez)
Organizations that raise money, often from donations, and then uses the money to help the needy or other good causes.

degrade (dih-GRAYD)
Rot, break down, or fall apart.

environmentally friendly
(in-vy-run-MEN-tul-ee FREND-lee)
Not damaging to the air, land, rivers, lakes, and oceans, or to plants and animals.

fragrant (FRAY-grint)
Having a sweet or pleasant smell.

herbs (ERBZ)
Plants that usually have a strong but pleasant smell, which are used in cooking and sometimes in medicines and perfumes.

landfills (LAND-filz)
A large site where garbage is dumped and buried.

manufacture
(man-yuh-FAK-cher)
Make a product on a large scale, usually using machines.

recycle (ree-SY-kul)
Turn used materials into new products.

unique (yoo-NEEK)
One of a kind.

upcycled (UP-sy-kuld)
Turned into something new
that has value and is often
environmentally friendly.

WEBSITES

Due to the changing nature
of Internet links, PowerKids Press
has developed an online list of websites
related to the subject of this book.
This site is updated regularly. Please use
this link to access the list:

www.powerkidslinks.com/ftt/nature/

READ MORE

Close, Edward. *What Do We Do with Trash?* Discovery Education: The Environment. New York: PowerKids Press, 2012.

Luxbacher, Irene. *The Jumbo Book of Outdoor Art*. Jumbo Books Series. Toronto: Kids Can Press, 2006.

Monaghan, Kimberly. *Organic Crafts: 75 Earth-Friendly Art Activities*. Chicago: Chicago Review Press, 2007.

INDEX